Alfonsocasas

FREDDIE
Mercury
an
Illustrated Life

University of Texas Press ✦ Austin

alfonsocasas

FREDDIE MERCURY

an Illustrated Life

First Edition: October 2018
© 2018 by Alfonso Casas

© 2018 for the Spanish-language edition throughout the world:
Penguin Random House Grupo Editorial, S.A.U.
Travessera de Gràcia, 47-49. 08021 Barcelona

First University of Texas Press edition, 2020
English translation © 2020 by Ned Sublette

Requests for permission to reproduce material
from this work should be sent to:
Permissions
University of Texas Press
P.O. Box 7819
Austin, TX 78713-7819
utpress.utexas.edu/rp-form

♾ The paper used in this book meets the minimum requirements of
ANSI/NISO Z39.48-1992 (R1997) (Permanence of Paper).

Library of Congress Cataloging-in-Publication Data

Names: Casas, Alfonso, author. | Sublette, Ned, 1951–, translator.
Title: Freddie Mercury : an illustrated life / Alfonso Casas ; translated from the Spanish by
Ned Sublette.
Other titles: Freddie Mercury, una biografía. English
Description: First University of Texas Press edition. | Austin : University of Texas Press, 2020. |
Includes bibliographical references.
Identifiers: LCCN 2019034386
    ISBN 978-1-4773-2063-1 (cloth)
    ISBN 978-1-4773-2126-3 (library ebook)
    ISBN 978-1-4773-2127-0 (non-library ebook)
Subjects: LCSH: Mercury, Freddie. | Queen (Musical group) | Rock musicians—England—
Biography. | Singers—England—Biography. | Gay men—England—Biography.
Classification: LCC ML420.M389 C3713 2020 | DDC 782.42166092 [B]—dc23
LC record available at https://lccn.loc.gov/2019034386

doi:10.7560/320631

He lived life to the full. He devoured life. He celebrated every minute. And, like a great comet, he left a luminous trail which will sparkle for many a generation to come.

—BRIAN MAY, 2011

PROLOGUE

I can't tell you what my favorite movie is, or what book I'd take to a desert island. But if you ask me my favorite song, no problem.

My first contact with this particular song was in the mid-'90s, in a cover version by an R&B group. Access to information was not yet a click away (I feel a little older as I write this), so it took me a while to figure out that "Bohemian Rhapsody" was originally done by a group called . . .

Queen. From that moment on, the more I've listened to Queen—and to its lead singer, Freddie Mercury—the greater the impact they've had, not only on the music you hear on the radio, but in my life in general. I'd already sung "We Are the Champions" at a ballgame. I'd stomped the floor and clapped my hands to the rhythm of "We Will Rock You." Years before that, I'd been excited about "Who Wants to Live Forever." Even Freddie Mercury's iconic look was already carved into my brain and I didn't know it. It was like a puzzle missing only one piece.

That piece was Queen. Bit by bit I came to understand that the group's importance transcended musical boundaries. All the members of Queen, and especially Freddie Mercury, offer us a way to understand a moment when everything seemed new and fascinating.

Many changes came in the Queen years, not all of them good. But even in the darkest moments of the '70s and '80s—foundational decades for our lives, even for those of us who came along later—the figure of Freddie Mercury blazed. Freddie lived like an authentic rock star, but not in the stereotypical way. Rock was a genre set in its ways, and he changed the rules of the game, breaking all the barriers that supposedly existed. His iconic mustache, his tight shorts, his leather jackets weren't only aesthetic decisions. They broke with the classic rock-star model. He was an example of how a person can triumph while—or precisely because of—transgressing social norms. Because where others were simply eccentric, Freddie Mercury was free.

Freddie never used his private life as a gimmick to sell records. He was jealous of his privacy, so in a sense the person and the persona developed along separate paths. And although, as the voice of Queen, Freddie had a space on the Olympus of (rock) gods, reserved for only a few, there was another Freddie whose fears and desires were those of mere mortals. Behind the leader of one of the world's all-time most successful rock bands was a timid person, with an inner life that he struggled both to reveal and to hide.

This book will not take a deep dive into Freddie Mercury's private life, although in its pages details appear that help us understand him. Nor is it a reference book about Queen, though you'll find many facts about the group in it. At times Freddie's compositions seem to tell us about his personal life and at times his personal life can be reconstructed through his music, blurring the border between the two. That is precisely the intention of this book: to draw, literally and metaphorically, a portrait of the formidable figure that is Freddie Mercury. It offers a modest homage to what his music and his person signified to many, and signify still, even for those of us who were not born Queen fans, but will die Queen fans.

TABLE OF CONTENTS

"Bohemian Rhapsody," one of Freddie Mercury's best-known compositions, shattered the then-existing templates of rock—not only for its length (almost six minutes) but also for its structure, in which there is no chorus. Nothing in "Bohemian Rhapsody" repeats; everything in it is new. It moves perpetually forward, the way Freddie's life did.

Each chapter of this book echoes a section of that megahit, as if his life and his most famous songs flowed in parallel. Like its author, "Bohemian Rhapsody" went out of the way to find its way.

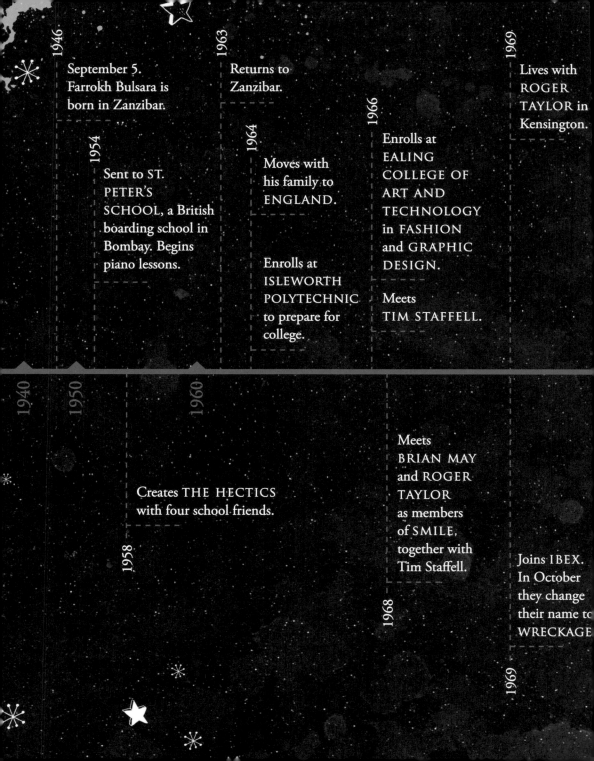

1946

September 5. Farrokh Bulsara is born in Zanzibar.

1954

Sent to ST. PETER'S SCHOOL, a British boarding school in Bombay. Begins piano lessons.

1963

Returns to Zanzibar.

1964

Moves with his family to ENGLAND.

Enrolls at ISLEWORTH POLYTECHNIC to prepare for college.

1966

Enrolls at EALING COLLEGE OF ART AND TECHNOLOGY in FASHION and GRAPHIC DESIGN.

Meets TIM STAFFELL.

1969

Lives with ROGER TAYLOR in Kensington.

1940

1950

1960

Creates THE HECTICS with four school friends.

1958

Meets BRIAN MAY and ROGER TAYLOR as members of SMILE, together with Tim Staffell.

1968

Joins IBEX. In October they change their name to WRECKAGE

1969

1970

Graduates in graphic arts and design.

Begins a relationship with MARY AUSTIN.

Begins to call himself FREDDIE MERCURY.

1972

Freddie designs QUEEN'S logo.

1975

Unfaithful to Mary Austin with David Minns.

1976

Ends his relationship with Mary Austin.

1970

Leaves WRECKAGE, joins SOUR MILK SEA.

Tim Staffell leaves SMILE and Freddie joins the group. They change their name to QUEEN.

1971

JOHN DEACON joins the group.

QUEEN records their first demos.

1973

First QUEEN album.

First tour, opening for MOTT THE HOOPLE.

1974

Release of QUEEN II (March).

Release of SHEER HEART ATTACK (November).

1975

Release of the single "BOHEMIAN RHAPSODY."

And the album A NIGHT AT THE OPERA.

1976

Release of A DAY AT THE RACES.

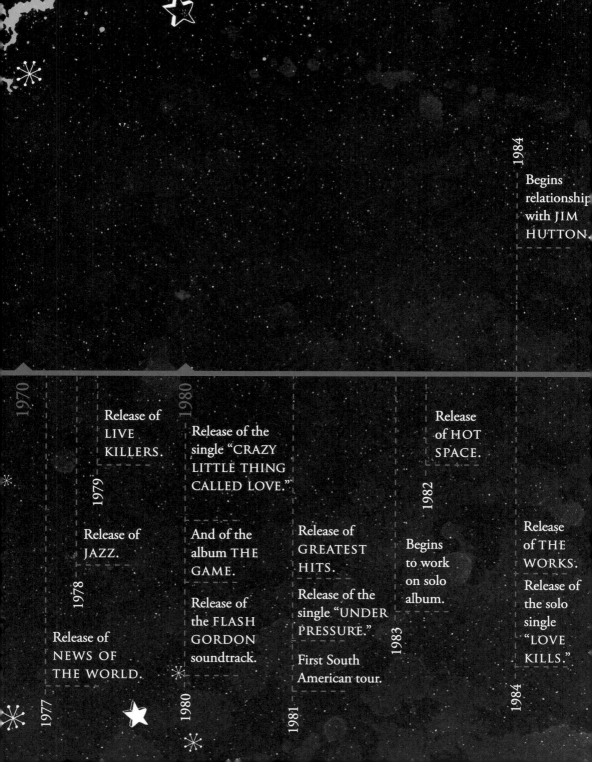

1984

Begins
relationship
with JIM
HUTTON.

1970

1980

1979

Release of
LIVE
KILLERS.

Release of the
single "CRAZY
LITTLE THING
CALLED LOVE."

Release
of HOT
SPACE.

1982

1978

Release of
JAZZ.

And of the
album THE
GAME.

Release of
GREATEST
HITS.

Begins
to work
on solo
album.

Release
of THE
WORKS.

Release of
NEWS OF
THE WORLD.

Release of
the FLASH
GORDON
soundtrack.

Release of the
single "UNDER
PRESSURE."

First South
American tour.

1983

Release of
the solo
single
"LOVE
KILLS."

1977

1980

1981

1984

1985

1987

Diagnosed with AIDS.

Meets MONTSERRAT CABALLÉ.

1991

November 22: Freddie releases official communication about his illness.

November 24: Freddie Mercury dies in London.

Thirty-ninth birthday party.

1988

Queen's songs begin listing all four members as authors.

1990

Release of the solo album MR. BAD GUY.

Records three songs for the musical TIME.

Release of the album BARCELONA with MONTSERRAT CABALLÉ.

Release of MADE IN HEAVEN.

Queen performs at LIVE AID.

Release of A KIND OF MAGIC.

1988

1995

Release of INNUENDO (February).

1985

Last QUEEN tour with FREDDIE MERCURY.

Release of the single "THE GREAT PRETENDER."

1991

Release of THE MIRACLE.

1986

1987

1989

INTRO

Freddie Mercury was born three times at least.

That might seem like a strange way to begin, but that's how Freddie was. Of the many stories written about him throughout his life, some are true and some definitely are not. But in all of the tellings he is memorable.

The first time he was born, on September 5, 1946, was in Stone Town, one of the principal cities of Zanzibar. His name was Farrokh Bulsara, the son of Bomi and Jer Bulsara.

The boy seemed destined for stardom from birth. One of the few tangible connections to him that can be found in Stone Town today is a baby picture. The portrait, which won a photography contest, is still in the window of the photo studio where it was taken—a rare memento of him in his hometown, along with some clippings and photos that decorate the entryway to the house where he spent his first years.

Farrokh was very close to his younger sister, Kashmira, in his childhood years. They were raised in one of the oldest existing religious beliefs—the Persian faith of Zoroastrianism, among whose most important precepts is to celebrate life. The child Farrokh understood this perfectly, although later in life the more restrictive and traditional side of the religion would enter into direct conflict with his way of living.

Zanzibar was a paradisiacal place in those years, but still the Bulsara children always gazed beyond the island's limits, listening to pop music and reading Western fashion magazines, arriving months after they were published.

There was a big world out there. It wouldn't take Farrokh long to find it.

Farrokh left Zanzibar for the first time in the summer of 1954, when his parents decided he should continue his education where his aunt and grandmother lived, near Bombay (Mumbai). It was they who detected the boy's artistic precociousness, and gave him the opportunity to explore it. Oil painting was followed by piano classes. He could play songs he'd heard on the radio without any sheet music in front of him, amazing his teacher.

Before long he was forming his first music group, together with three friends at St. Peter's, the boarding school where he studied in the years leading up to his adolescence. The Hectics, as they were called, played versions of songs by the most famous artists of the day—Buddy Holly, Elvis Presley.

At school, the diminutive Farrokh was introverted. He was a good student who didn't stand out too much (though his teeth did, much to his chagrin, making him the object of some mockery). On stage, though, he seemed like someone else. The Farrokh who played Cliff Richard songs on the piano was a brave boy, a more confident version of himself. That duality was with him all his life: timid person/audacious persona.

When he decided that his friends should call him Freddie, his new name quickly spread outside the gates of St. Peter's and even to his family members. Being Freddie gave Farrokh a more expansive personality, opening up a new, more daring, more theatrical attitude beneath the thin disguise. By then he was already ending his phrases with the word *darling*, something scandalous in that time and place, but which coming from him seemed spontaneous and natural. As Freddie demonstrated repeatedly in the (few) interviews he gave, he never stopped using that term.

Together with the Hectics, Farrokh Bulsara had been born again. This time his name was Freddie.

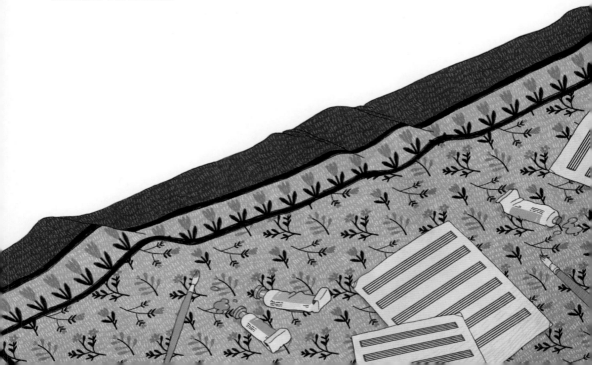

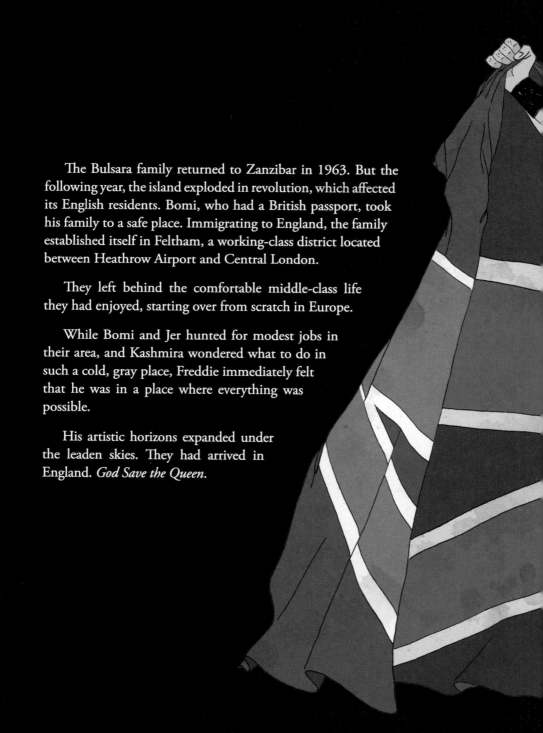

The Bulsara family returned to Zanzibar in 1963. But the following year, the island exploded in revolution, which affected its English residents. Bomi, who had a British passport, took his family to a safe place. Immigrating to England, the family established itself in Feltham, a working-class district located between Heathrow Airport and Central London.

They left behind the comfortable middle-class life they had enjoyed, starting over from scratch in Europe.

While Bomi and Jer hunted for modest jobs in their area, and Kashmira wondered what to do in such a cold, gray place, Freddie immediately felt that he was in a place where everything was possible.

His artistic horizons expanded under the leaden skies. They had arrived in England. *God Save the Queen.*

While he helped out the family with different jobs, Freddie prepared to enter the Ealing School of Art in London. This was something he wanted not only in order to continue his art studies (his family was not in agreement), but for another, even more important, reason: the musical environment within its walls.

Under the influence of occidental culture, Freddie began modifying his physical appearance, passing from a polished, formal aesthetic to one more in tune with the young Brits of his time. Although his mother was not pleased with his

long hair, there was no way for her to restrain Freddie's desire to fit into his new reality.

It wasn't hard for him to shine at school, and in 1966 he matriculated at Ealing, where he studied fashion design before moving over to graphic design. In those years he met Tim Staffell, a schoolmate who harmonized with him when they sang in the school's bathroom, making the space reverberate and prefiguring what everyone would in time come to know as the Queen sound.

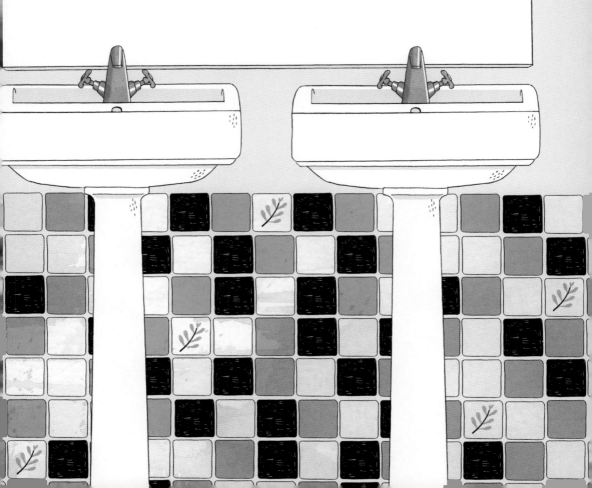

BALLAD

Freddie's friend Tim played bass and sang lead for a group called Smile. The guitarist, Brian May, was a physics and astronomy student, and the drummer, Roger Taylor, was studying to be an odontologist. Their classic rock fascinated Freddie from the first gig he saw, and he followed them wherever they played, making friends with them and generally functioning as their number one fan.

In 1969, Freddie and Roger Taylor moved into a building near the Kensington Market, where they shared a flat and together ran a small secondhand clothes shop. Although their store was popular with local kids, the real fashion hotspot was a store called Biba, which was frequented by the members of Smile not only for its merchandise but also for its compelling young saleswoman, Mary Austin.

Brian took Mary out a couple of times, but nothing happened between them. Freddie also took an interest in Mary, but he was a regular at the store for six months before he dared to ask her out.

Five months later, Mary and Freddie were living together. It lasted for six years—not only one of Freddie's longest relationships, but also one of his most consequential.

By then music had become Freddie's priority, and his other studies were suffering as a consequence. His new idol was Jimi Hendrix, whose picture he sketched constantly. Admiring not only Hendrix's musical talent but also his ability to grab the attention of the public, he realized that if he wanted to be a successful singer, his command of spectacle would be as important as his voice.

While he continued searching for his own style, Freddie sang with various groups, including Ibex (later Wreckage). According to the group's bassist, John Taylor, Bulsara was nicknamed "The Queen" within the group because of his mannerisms. Freddie's revenge wasn't long in coming: he would appropriate the word and invest it with new significance, converting what others saw as a flaw into his greatest virtue.

The Queen was going to be much bigger than them, *darling*.

Tim Staffell quit Smile in 1970, leaving Brian and Roger without a singer. Freddie was a singer without a group. It didn't take a genius to solve the puzzle. Freddie named the new band Queen.

By that time, Freddie had decided to change his last name from Bulsara to Mercury. Much has been written about this decision, but Brian May attributed it to one of the first verses Freddie wrote: "Mother Mercury, look what they've done to me," in his song "My Fairy King." Freddie insisted that it was an homage to Mercury, the messenger of the gods.

If the spirit of Farrokh Bulsara still lurked within him, timid and withdrawn, no one would know. He'd been reborn, again. This time his name was Freddie Mercury.

At some point, an amateur band faces a moment of truth. If they don't get some recognition that inspires them to continue, they have to choose whether to keep trying or let it go. That moment came for the members of Queen when they finished their studies: bet on music, or dedicate themselves to the professions they'd been studying to enter.

Freddie was clear: he wasn't going to be a rock star, he was going to be a legend.

Queen decided to polish their style and look for a record deal. They kept writing songs and playing live whenever someone would let them. That was when the tight leather pants and black painted fingernails appeared, adding a glam aesthetic to the band's presentation. They frightened off a couple of bassists before the shy John Deacon joined in 1971, completing the original lineup of Queen, which would last for more than twenty years.

It wasn't until 1972 that producers started to notice them, after they played a cover of "Big Spender" at one of their gigs. It was the perfect showcase of what made Queen stand out: while other rock bands played versions of Led Zeppelin and the like, they mixed in Shirley Bassey songs. This attracted the attention of the executives at Trident, a company with its own state-of-the-art recording studio in the heart of London.

Always keen on drawing, Freddie was naturally the one to take charge of Queen's visual image. He designed a coat of arms that they used on every album: it depicts the four members' zodiac signs guarding the group's initial Q, while a phoenix towers over them all, its wings spread. Though officially representing the band's origins in the ashes of other groups like Wreckage and Smile, the phoenix could just as easily refer to Freddie's ability to reinvent himself.

Trident offered Queen a deal that included studio time—although they had to adjust their schedule around sessions by "real" stars—and the cost of instruments and support personnel. The excited band didn't pay attention to the contractual details: except for a small weekly allowance, nobody would get any money until the whole investment was recouped.

During the sessions, Freddie managed to record two numbers for a project being put together at the studio under the name of Larry Lurex. The idea never went anywhere, but over time both songs became fan curiosities.

Pursuant to a deal Trident made with EMI, Queen's eponymous debut was released worldwide in July 1973. Neither the album nor the single, "Keep Yourself Alive," made the charts. The record didn't remotely match Freddie's expectations, and it didn't make him into the rock star he wanted to be. Becoming a legend would have to wait a little longer.

While their underpromoted first album was still new, the members of Queen started working on tunes for a new record. This time around, the material wasn't rescued from the ashes of Smile and Wreckage but was created specifically for the band. In it, Freddie Mercury's sonic signature began to emerge: a certain harmonic style, along with a sense of how to layer tracks.

Although today Queen seems like an inoffensive name, at the time it was an edgy choice. Whenever the group was asked about it, their answer was always the same: Queen was a majestic name, easy to remember, glamorous and universal. They never denied the name's connotation of gayness, but that was only one interpretation of it. They let the work speak for itself.

Although Queen had had some success opening for Mott the Hoople on a nationwide tour, the group's popularity grew exponentially when they made their first TV appearance, on *Top of the Pops*. They played "Seven Seas of Rhye," the first single from their new album, and although they weren't allowed to play it live, the group took full advantage of the opportunity to be seen by a mass audience, and that audience liked them.

The power of the tube was obvious when *Queen II* went to number five on the British charts upon its release in March 1974, with their first album now charting as well.

The (other) members of Queen

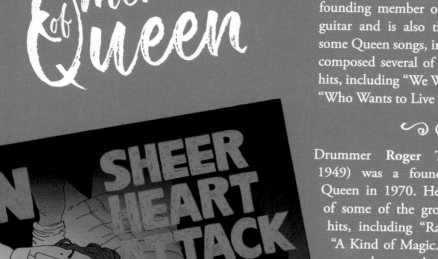

Brian May (born in Hampton, 1947) was, together with Tim Staffell, an original member of Smile. May, a founding member of the group, plays guitar and is also the lead singer on some Queen songs, including "'39." He composed several of the band's biggest hits, including "We Will Rock You" and "Who Wants to Live Forever?"

Drummer **Roger Taylor** (Norfolk, 1949) was a founding member of Queen in 1970. He is the composer of some of the group's number one hits, including "Radio Ga Ga" and "A Kind of Magic." He and Freddie seemed to understand each other well. Making a cameo appearance as a chorus singer, he appeared in the video of Freddie's solo single "The Great Pretender."

Bassist **John Deacon** (Leicester, 1951) was the last to join the band, in 1971. At one time he was considered Queen's "secret weapon" for his ability to write hits like "Another One Bites the Dust" and "I Want to Break Free." He played bass for Freddie on *Barcelona*, Freddie's second album without Queen.

As Queen moved toward stardom, the group tried to define a look that was a mixture of glam rock and fairy tales (the latter being an obsession of Freddie's in those days, as his song titles show). Freddie knew that in order to be memorable, Queen had to stand out. If some thought them exaggerated and pretentious, at least no one would remain indifferent. As he took charge of the theatrical side—sets, costumes, and all the trappings of showbiz—the group began working with designer Zandra Rhodes, who interpreted Freddie's ideas and created some of the band's best-known costumes of the '70s.

In the summer of 1974 they began recording the album *Sheer Heart Attack*, which contained their first massive hit single: "Killer Queen," today considered the touchstone of the Queen sound. It brought Freddie his first major recognition as a composer, the Ivor Novello prize, in 1975.

But in spite of topping the charts and touring in the US, Europe, and Japan, there was no money coming in, and the unhappy band hired a lawyer to negotiate their escape from Trident. From then on, the members of Queen took charge of their own music, taking the impresarial dimension into careful account.

They hired a manager: John Reid, who was working with Freddie's friend Elton John. The first thing he did was tell them, "Go make the best record you can, I'll take care of the rest." A few months later, he'd be sorry he said that.

According to John Reid, the first time he visited Freddie at home, he realized to his surprise that behind the extroverted glam-rock pose was a quiet young man who lived surrounded by cats, listening to Liza Minnelli.

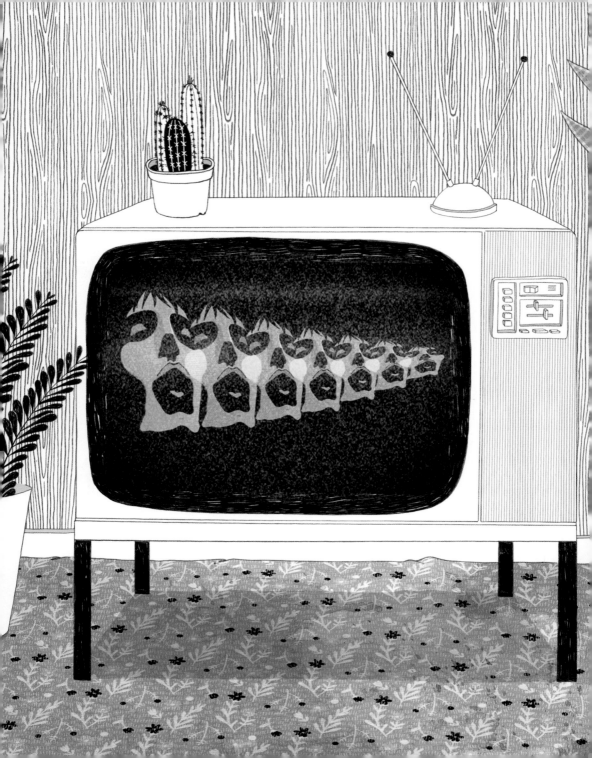

A Night at the Opera, Queen's next album, was one of the most expensive album productions in history. Although it upset some critics to hear pop songs, heavy rock, operatic reminiscences, and '20s vaudeville touches all in the same album, the band had found its own recognizable style.

One of the reasons for the group's success was also a source of conflict: all four members of Queen were composers. Choosing which song would be the single not only meant choosing which song would be the hit (something very important at the level of ego), but also which composer would collect the most royalties.

But in spite of ego and money in the balance, the four musicians of Queen agreed that the first single from *A Night at the Opera* should be "Bohemian Rhapsody." Freddie's almost-six-minute composition represented everything Queen was at that moment: vocal harmonies multiplied out to infinity, colorful production, a guitar solo that would make rock history, and lyrics that still seem enigmatic today.

"Bohemian Rhapsody" spent nine weeks at number one on the British charts. It became one of the biggest-selling singles in history, beaten out only by Abba's "Mamma Mia." (Curiously, "Bohemian Rhapsody" includes the line "Oh mama mia, mama mia, mama mia, let me go.")

To promote the single, the group recorded a music videoclip—a then unusual medium—for *Top of the Pops*. The clip's director, Bruce Gowers, subsequently directed some seasons of *American Idol*. One of the losers during that show's eighth season was a young singer named Adam Lambert who, though he lost the competition, today travels with Queen as vocalist on their tours.

ALTHOUGH SOME SAY THAT THE SONG SPEAKS OF A CHARACTER WHO SELLS HIS SOUL TO THE DEVIL, AND OTHERS INSIST THAT ITS LYRICS ARE INSPIRED BY ALBERT CAMUS'S *THE STRANGER*, EVERYONE SEEMS TO AGREE THAT "BOHEMIAN RHAPSODY" CONTAINS AUTOBIOGRAPHICAL MATERIAL ABOUT THE SINGER, ALTHOUGH HE NEVER GAVE ANY KIND OF OFFICIAL STATEMENT ABOUT IT.

THE STRANGER ALBERT CAMUS

IN 1975, FREDDIE HAD A CONVERSATION WITH MAR[Y] AUSTIN WHERE HE CONFES[SED] TO BEING UNFAITHFUL TO H[ER] WHILE OPENING UP TO HE[R] ABOUT HIS HOMOSEXUALIT[Y]

THIS KILLS THE MAN THAT THE SONG'S NARRATOR HAD PREVIOUSLY BEEN, AND BEGINS AN EMOTIONAL QUEST IN SEARCH OF A NEW SELF.

"MAMA, JUST KILLED A MAN PUT A GUN AGAINST HIS HEAD PULLED MY TRIGGER NOW HE'S DEAD."

DURING THIS JOURNEY HE HAS TO CONFRONT HIS OWN SELF-JUDGMENT AS WELL AS THE JUDGMENT OF OTHERS.

"HE'S JUST A POOR BOY FROM A POOR FAMILY SPARE HIM HIS LIFE FROM THIS MONSTROSITY."

By 1976 Queen's success was worldwide. Fame and money had arrived at last, but the increased popularity coincided with a difficult moment in Freddie's personal life, when his relationship with Mary Austin ended.

Although Farrokh Bulsara had authoritatively created the persona of Freddie Mercury, it was only a matter of time before rips appeared in the rock-star costume he had carefully sewn. In much the same way that he stacked vocal harmonies in the studio, he had constructed so many layers of himself that they became an impenetrable barrier between the world and the real Freddie.

He wasn't being truthful—neither with himself nor with Mary, which pained him. Their relationship had changed in recent years, contaminated by rumors of infidelity and half-truths, so that when Freddie came out to Mary about his bisexuality, the truth was easier to accept than the doubts and fears.

Mary saw it as the first step in accepting his homosexuality. Not wanting to deny the real Freddie, she was supportive. Although the nature of their relationship changed, their love remained until the end. No other lover was as important in the life of Freddie as Mary. In various interviews he described her as the only person he could confide in. For her he composed the song "Love of My Life."

Freddie now lived a different life, one in which he was more honest with himself and with those around him. New, long-lasting friendships began, like those with the comic Kenny Everett or the British musician and producer Dave Clark, to whom he was always very close.

He was ready to enjoy what his new rock-star status could offer him, especially on the economic side. Not everyone was supportive: when *A Day at the Races* was released in 1976, the press criticized his lightweight songs that spoke of glamorous romances, dinners at the Ritz, and other rich people's problems. But since the music press had never treated Queen very well, the group's members decided to let the public have the last word.

While they were promoting the record, Freddie spoke with an interviewer from *NME* in which, after being asked his influences, he said that his intention was to bring "ballet to the masses." The article ran with the headline: *Is this man a prat* [idiot]? From then on, Freddie decided to give as few interviews as possible and stay out of public view.

Is this man a prat?

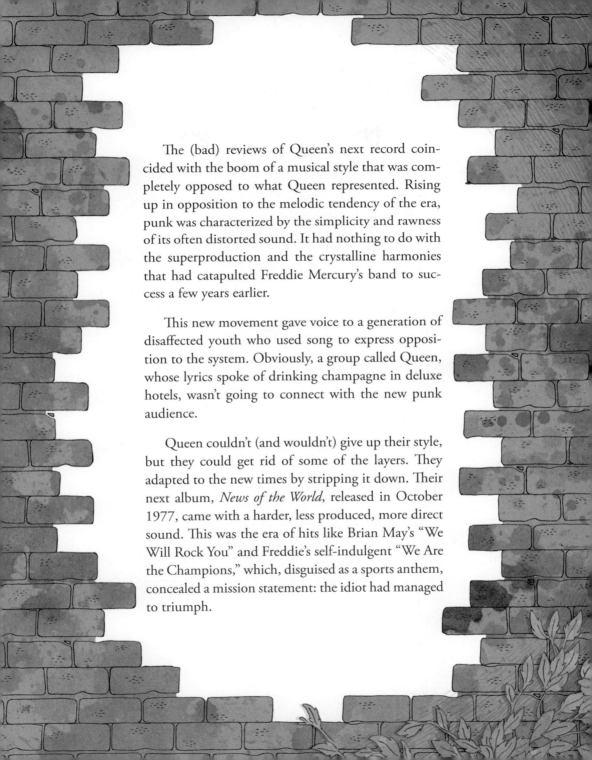

The (bad) reviews of Queen's next record coincided with the boom of a musical style that was completely opposed to what Queen represented. Rising up in opposition to the melodic tendency of the era, punk was characterized by the simplicity and rawness of its often distorted sound. It had nothing to do with the superproduction and the crystalline harmonies that had catapulted Freddie Mercury's band to success a few years earlier.

This new movement gave voice to a generation of disaffected youth who used song to express opposition to the system. Obviously, a group called Queen, whose lyrics spoke of drinking champagne in deluxe hotels, wasn't going to connect with the new punk audience.

Queen couldn't (and wouldn't) give up their style, but they could get rid of some of the layers. They adapted to the new times by stripping it down. Their next album, *News of the World*, released in October 1977, came with a harder, less produced, more direct sound. This was the era of hits like Brian May's "We Will Rock You" and Freddie's self-indulgent "We Are the Champions," which, disguised as a sports anthem, concealed a mission statement: the idiot had managed to triumph.

After a successful tour in America (where punk had made less of an impact), in the summer of 1978, the band took a few months off to rest and write their next record.

Those months were for Freddie the beginning of the craziest period of his life, marked by excesses and the discovery (and enjoyment) of his own sexuality. As part of a cycle that had begun in his childhood, Freddie broke free of the chrysalis he'd been growing in. It was time to enjoy his dazzling new wings.

Don't stop me now

After the release of *Jazz*, tired of the press's constant invasions of his privacy, Freddie Mercury decided to spend some time away from England. He wanted to experiment, have fun, and live this new stage of his life, and New York was the perfect city for that. There he could have a certain anonymity while still enjoying all the advantages of big-stardom. In the Big Apple, Freddie had a string of lovers, none of whom stayed more than one night. One night he met Joe Fanelli, a cook whom he wound up hiring as a chef for his house in England.

As the boundary between night and day became blurred, Freddie found he liked walking on the wild side. He continued being the timid boy who covered his mouth out of embarrassment when he laughed, but with alcohol and other excesses taking away his inhibitions, he was a night creature, with no intention of returning to his cage.

CRAZY LITTLE THING CALLED LOVE

PETER, BRING ME THE GUITAR, FAST!

In June 1979 the group went to Munich to record a new album, and Freddie wrote "Crazy Little Thing Called Love" in his hotel bathtub. Recalling the sound of '50s Elvis, it became his first number one hit in the US.

Freddie had told his now ex-manager, John Reid, that the band needed someone to go with them on their tours to make sure they got what they needed. John thought he had the ideal candidate: Paul Prenter. Brian, John, and Roger quickly dispensed with his services (Roger later said he considered Prenter "the worst possible influence"), but Freddie depended on him to be his personal assistant. Paul Prenter's job was to make everything easy for Freddie. He became Freddie's sidekick from night until morning, and exactly at those hours.

The '80s arrived, and with them Queen's eighth album, *The Game*, whose fourth single was chosen by Michael Jackson; he told them backstage at one of their shows that it would be crazy not to put out "Another One Bites the Dust" as a single.

The band members weren't so sure; John Deacon's song had almost been left off the album. But Michael's hunch was right: it became their second number one single in the US and sold seven million copies worldwide.

With their latest single at number one around the world, and with their records racking up millions of units, Queen was the most popular band on the planet. But success is easier to achieve than to keep, and the members of Queen knew that their reign was ephemeral: they had displaced another band from the number one spot, and someone else would knock them off.

But, for the moment, Queen had the world at its feet.

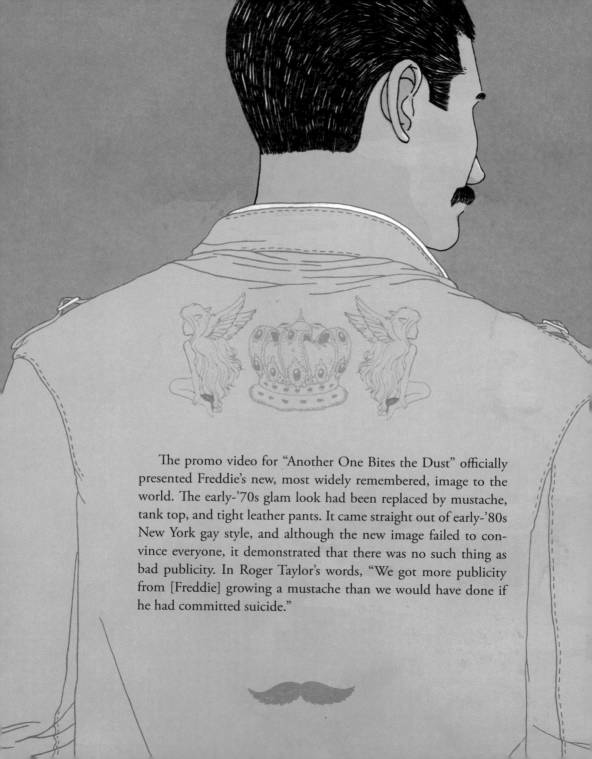

The promo video for "Another One Bites the Dust" officially presented Freddie's new, most widely remembered, image to the world. The early-'70s glam look had been replaced by mustache, tank top, and tight leather pants. It came straight out of early-'80s New York gay style, and although the new image failed to convince everyone, it demonstrated that there was no such thing as bad publicity. In Roger Taylor's words, "We got more publicity from [Freddie] growing a mustache than we would have done if he had committed suicide."

Freddie's
MAKEOVERS

Although in the collective imaginary Freddie Mercury always had (and will have) a mustache and short hair, that was only his most recognizable look. Here are some of the styles he wore over the course of his life.

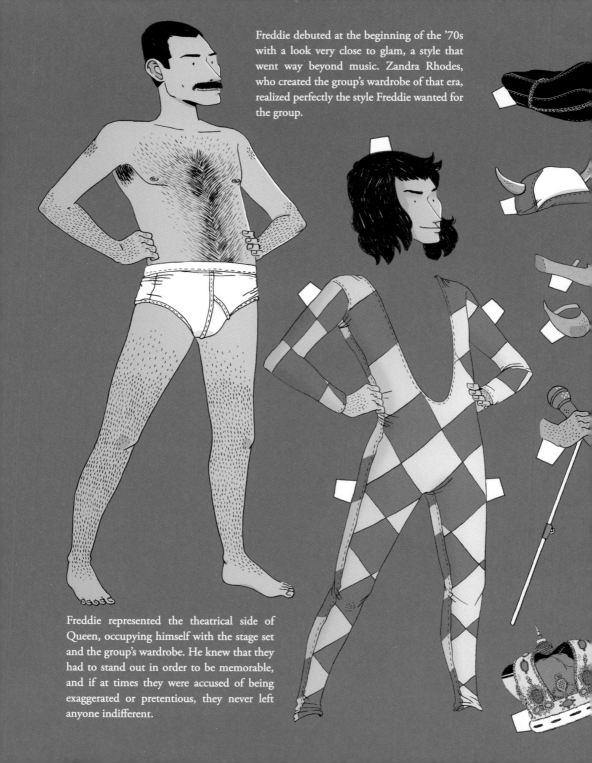

Freddie debuted at the beginning of the '70s with a look very close to glam, a style that went way beyond music. Zandra Rhodes, who created the group's wardrobe of that era, realized perfectly the style Freddie wanted for the group.

Freddie represented the theatrical side of Queen, occupying himself with the stage set and the group's wardrobe. He knew that they had to stand out in order to be memorable, and if at times they were accused of being exaggerated or pretentious, they never left anyone indifferent.

At the end of the '70s Freddie had cut his hair and had incorporated leather as the basis of his look. The '80s brought his most recognizable images: the mustache, the tight T-shirts, the famous yellow jacket. They remain forever engraved in our memories.

In the final stage of his life, Freddie set aside his eccentricities when he dressed. He began to wear a suit (a bright-colored satin one, to be sure) and even shaved his mustache. In his last years he was sometimes seen with a beard, wearing simpler clothes. But his sense of elegance, which went beyond how he dressed, was with him to the end.

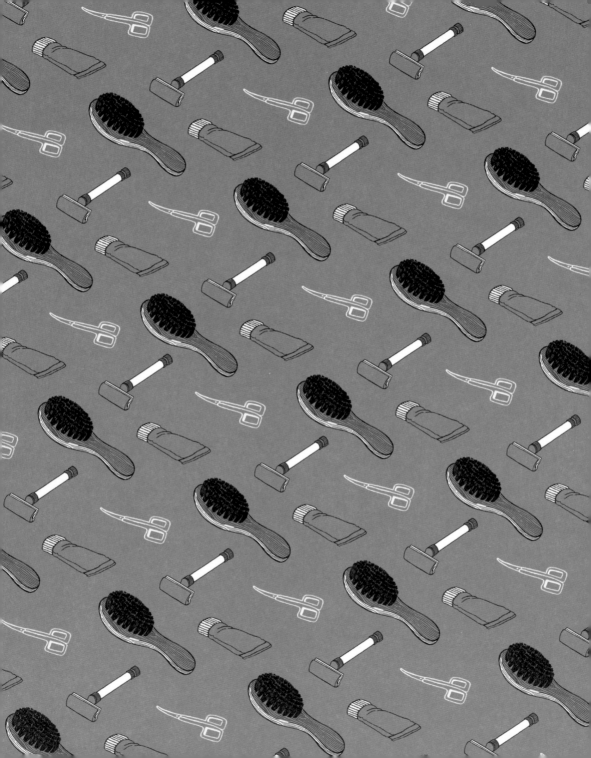

Freddie's nights in New York changed more than his look. They inspired a new interest in disco music. Paul Prenter, whose influence over him was growing, was in favor of a style closer to the electronic Donna Summer sound, seeing Queen's guitar-and-bass instrumentation as old-fashioned. Brian and Roger, who didn't trust Prenter at all, took his comments as undermining the essence of the group and the friendship of its members.

Still, emboldened by the massive success of "Another One Bites the Dust," they decided to go for more of a funk-disco sound in their album *Hot Space*, which came out in 1982. The music was so far from Roger and Brian's taste that they didn't even play on some of the songs.

Some music critics said that the band was a latecomer to the disco style; Freddie argued that the album had come out too close to the explosion of funk. For whatever reason, the album flopped in the stores, and only stayed afloat thanks to "Under Pressure," the single they recorded with David Bowie, which was a hit in England.

The failure of *Hot Space* was a shock for the group. It brought to light everything that was separating them, which at that moment was more than what was holding them together. Their conflicts, which usually remained on a professional level—something that, in a way, ultimately made their songs better—were no secret, but on occasion they crossed the line into the personal.

They had good relations with each other, but Freddie was always honest about the fact that Queen was a musical group, not a family. When they weren't touring or recording for months on end, they didn't spend time together. Each of the four took his own responsibility for separating his personal from his professional life.

Moreover, by that time Freddie was living a lifestyle that was totally alien to the rest of the members of Queen. Even on tour, they had stopped sharing moments offstage. This was in part the handiwork of Paul Prenter, who always seemed to make an "alternative" plan for Freddie, different from that of the group.

Having chalked up their worst sales figures and less united than ever, Queen found itself navigating its biggest crisis. Instead of breaking up definitively, the group decided to take some time off to start solo projects.

GUITAR SOLO

The news of Freddie Mercury's forthcoming first solo album caused a buzz in the music press. Both Roger and Brian had already developed their own projects when CBS, awash in cash from sales of Michael Jackson's *Thriller* album, offered Freddie a generous advance for his first project ouside the umbrella of Queen. His bandmates were not pleased to learn that it was more than the advances they had received for Queen albums.

Freddie had never hidden his economic interest in making a solo record. But beyond material compensation, he wanted to put out some songs under his name, and he wanted to keep investigating the musical line he'd begun with *Hot Space*.

At the beginning of 1983, Freddie starting working on tunes for the album at Munich's Musicland. At one point he'd planned to make the solo project an opportunity to do collaborations with other singers. He recorded some demos with Rod Stewart and Michael Jackson, with whom he worked on three songs. None of those collaborations materialized on the new album, although one of the songs he recorded with Michael came out years later on a Queen compilation.

Despite the musical and economic possibilities these collaborations might have offered, Freddie realized that coordinating a record with so many different egos on it would be a more titanic job than controlling only his own, so in the end he chose to make the record completely solo. This gave him total freedom of movement, but it also meant that he was the only one responsible for the end product.

But the months passed, and the ideas weren't flowing. Freddie's solo record was stuck. Roger Taylor stopped in at Musicland from time to time to try to help him, but the record failed to move forward. Freddie had underestimated the work it took to make a hit, even more so without collaborators.

Nor did being in Munich help. Away from the eyes of the press and the fans that swarmed him in London, Freddie could enjoy himself in anonymity. Together with Austrian actress Barbara Valentin, his tireless party companion of those years, he became a fixture in the local nightlife. Barbara and Freddie shared a bed, lovers, and infinite nights during their stay in Munich, even while Freddie carried on a relationship with Winnie Kirchberger, a German restauranteur who didn't speak English.

That summer, Queen received an offer to compose the music for a new movie. It would be their second, since they had already composed the score and main theme for Dino de Laurentis's 1980 film *Flash Gordon* while recording the album *The Game*. The band assembled in Los Angeles to begin creating songs for the movie, but they ended up rejecting the offer: their comeback as a band couldn't be a third-party project. Instead, they took advantage of being back together to start working on what would be their eleventh studio album, *The Works*.

The night life and its excesses seemed to take its toll on Freddie's spirit. He began to find the dynamic fatiguing. The other members of Queen had started their own families, who were waiting for them when they came back from long months on the road. They had created homes to return to, but Freddie hadn't. Although part of him wanted to find someone with whom he could share his life, in recent years he'd developed a suspicion of strangers, doubting whether their friendship could be sincere.

Secluded within himself and with his closest friends, Freddie decided to discharge Paul Prenter as his personal assistant, substituting Peter Freestone in his place. Phoebe, as he was known, was much more than an assistant; he became one of Freddie's closest friends until the end of his life.

In 1984 Queen ended a short hiatus with the album *The Works*, preceded by the single "Radio Ga Ga," their first big hit in years. There was controversy over the release of John Deacon's composition "I Want to Break Free," accompanied by a video in which all the members of the group cross-dressed. In the press, it was seen as a public declaration of Freddie's homosexuality, but it hadn't been his idea; it was Roger Taylor's girlfriend who had the idea for the video. A parody of the well-known English soap opera *Coronation Street*, it was received with laughter in Europe, but not in the United States.

With the strict mentality of the time, Americans had decided to overlook the (more than evident) gay aesthetic that Freddie had been flaunting, but were not willing to compromise further. Maybe ambiguity could be allowed in other musical genres, but rock continued to be a territory where a (fragile) concept of masculinity had to prevail. MTV passed on the video, although they offered to shoot another for broadcast in the US, which the group flatly refused.

With "I Want to Break Free," Queen became a global hit once again, but they lost the United States forever.

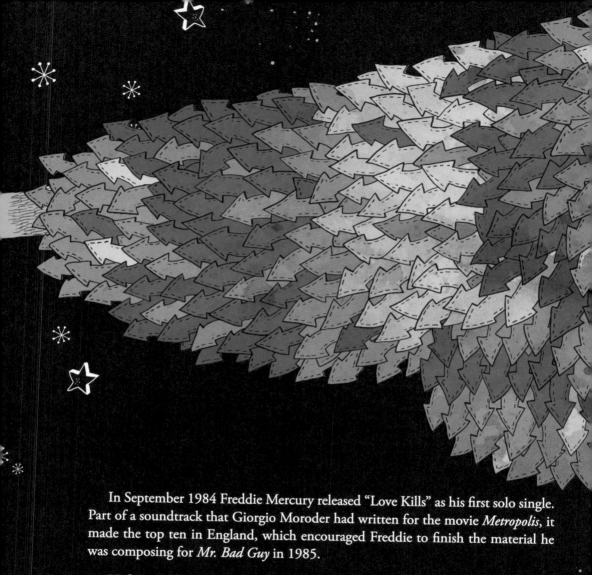

In September 1984 Freddie Mercury released "Love Kills" as his first solo single. Part of a soundtrack that Giorgio Moroder had written for the movie *Metropolis*, it made the top ten in England, which encouraged Freddie to finish the material he was composing for *Mr. Bad Guy* in 1985.

Unfortunately, *Mr. Bad Guy* was a disappointment—to Freddie, to the record company, and probably to Queen fans as well. Although the "four-headed hydra" (as Freddie sometimes called the members of Queen) contained egos that could be difficult to control, out of that friction came the group's biggest hits. Four heads were better than one, even if they were on a hydra.

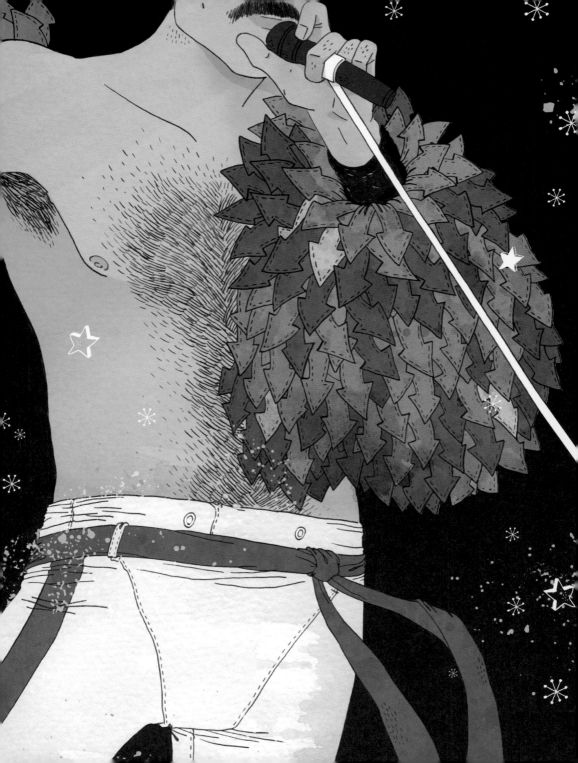

Although *Mr. Bad Guy* was a commercial failure, it had the saving grace of making Freddie understand how important it was for him, personally and professionally, to keep composing alongside the other members of Queen. Plus, he got to dedicate the record to the creatures he most loved in the world: his cats.

But his professional stumble hurt less than it might have, because at the end of 1984 Freddie had met Jim Hutton, a hairdresser with whom he achieved his dream of being in a couple. When Freddie met Jim in a bar in Kensington he tried to buy him a drink, but Jim refused the offer. Jim's friends advised him that the stranger inviting him to have a drink was none other than the rock star Freddie Mercury, but Jim had no idea who he was. That must have piqued Freddie's interest further, since he was distrustful of people who came on to him, fearing that they did it expecting something from him. The fact that Jim didn't know Freddie's public persona was the best possible signal, because it gave him the chance to get to know the person Freddie was in reality. But nothing got going that night.

They didn't meet again for eighteen months, although by then Freddie had investigated Jim's life a bit, and knew which places he frequented. That night, Freddie repeated the formula of trying to buy him a drink. After some risqué conversation, Jim and Freddie left the club together and never separated again. Many years before same-sex marriage was a legal possibility, Freddie always referred to Jim as his husband.

From then on, Freddie put an end to an era of addictions and promiscuity that had its own goodbye celebration in Munich, on his thirty-ninth birthday. It was the last excess Freddie Mercury permitted himself. The party attracted a diverse collection of the city's personalities and provided the backdrop for the promotional videoclip of his song "Living on My Own."

In the mid-'80s, neither Freddie Mercury nor the other members of Queen were at the top of the pop charts. Their solo records hadn't worked out the way they hoped and their only worldwide radio hit in four years had been "Radio Ga Ga." Perhaps the magic of Queen was gone. Was it the moment to break the group up definitively?

When, in the summer of 1985, Bob Geldof invited Queen to perform at a benefit concert, neither Freddie nor the rest of the group imagined that it would transform everything. With concurrent concerts in England and the United States to raise funds to combat hunger and poverty in Africa, Live Aid was going to be the most ambitious musical event in history. The concert would be broadcast internationally, with a potential audience of two billion people. Before the event, British and American stars had come together to record two benefit singles: the British song "Do They Know It's Christmas?" and the American single "We Are the World." Both sold massively, indicating that the concert would be the happening of the year.

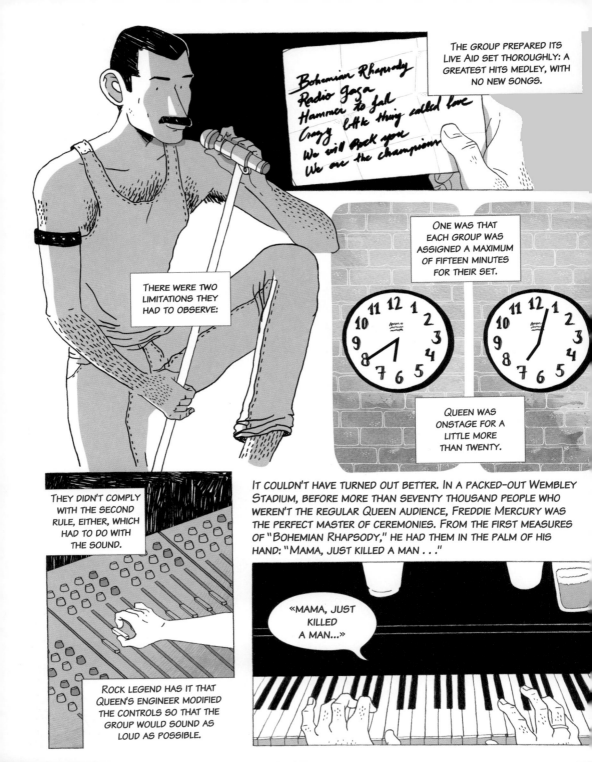

THE GROUP PREPARED ITS LIVE AID SET THOROUGHLY: A GREATEST HITS MEDLEY, WITH NO NEW SONGS.

Bohemian Rhapsody
Radio Gaga
Hammer to fall
Crazy little thing called love
We will Rock you
We are the champions

THERE WERE TWO LIMITATIONS THEY HAD TO OBSERVE:

ONE WAS THAT EACH GROUP WAS ASSIGNED A MAXIMUM OF FIFTEEN MINUTES FOR THEIR SET.

QUEEN WAS ONSTAGE FOR A LITTLE MORE THAN TWENTY.

THEY DIDN'T COMPLY WITH THE SECOND RULE, EITHER, WHICH HAD TO DO WITH THE SOUND.

IT COULDN'T HAVE TURNED OUT BETTER. IN A PACKED-OUT WEMBLEY STADIUM, BEFORE MORE THAN SEVENTY THOUSAND PEOPLE WHO WEREN'T THE REGULAR QUEEN AUDIENCE, FREDDIE MERCURY WAS THE PERFECT MASTER OF CEREMONIES. FROM THE FIRST MEASURES OF "BOHEMIAN RHAPSODY," HE HAD THEM IN THE PALM OF HIS HAND: "MAMA, JUST KILLED A MAN . . ."

«MAMA, JUST KILLED A MAN...»

ROCK LEGEND HAS IT THAT QUEEN'S ENGINEER MODIFIED THE CONTROLS SO THAT THE GROUP WOULD SOUND AS LOUD AS POSSIBLE.

As 1986 came in, Freddie Mercury was living his life to the fullest. He had finally settled down, establishing a home in Garden Lodge, a luxurious house located in Kensington that Mary Austin had been tasked with finding for him. There he lived with his cats (whom he always called when he was on tour) and Jim Hutton, with whom he had found the stability he had always wanted. Moreover, his work with Queen had taken off again—the media refocusing on the group after Live Aid—while Freddie continued developing some solo projects on the side.

One of these personal projects was related to a musical called *Time*, written by his friend Dave Clark, which premiered in April of that year in the Dominion Theatre (the same theatre that, in the future, would be the home of the Queen musical for twelve years). Clark offered him the starring role in the show, but though Freddie passed on it, he wrote three songs for the soundtrack. One of those songs, also called "Time," was released as a single. Although the single didn't do much, it started Freddie working with producer Mike Moran, who would be important in Freddie's next projects.

Inspired by their enormously successful performance at Live Aid, the members of Queen decided to get together at Musicland studios to work on new material, some of which ultimately wound up on *A Kind of Magic*. That album included the hits "One Vision" and "Friends Will Be Friends," and featured the group's songs composed for the movie *Highlander*. In 1986 the album brought Queen back to number one in sales as they kicked off what they called the Magic Tour.

Freddie had for years been honing his skill of conquering an audience, and the band had plenty of experience in massive tours that combined pyrotechnics, light, and sound with solid onstage musical performance. Conceived for stadiums, the Magic Tour brought the group's concert career to a new level of critical and popular success—but, unfortunately, it was the group's last tour with all four members.

The idea had been to end the tour with two shows in Wembley Arena, but the tickets went so fast that they had to book another date in an even larger place. On August 9, 1986, Queen gave an outdoor concert in Knebworth Park, finishing the tour in front of 120,000 people.

That night Freddie had trouble keeping to the high standards of energy his public expected. Although there are those who say that he had a cold that night, his body was simply exhausted. During the tour, Freddie had been making noises about not continuing much longer on the road, joking that he was getting too old to jump around on stage. The rest of the group didn't take him too seriously, but when Freddie got off the stage at Knebworth Park, he vowed never to give another concert.

OPERA

At the end of 1986, a few days before Freddie and Jim left for a getaway to Japan, Freddie decided to go to a doctor for a physical exam. Somehow word of his medical appointment leaked to the press.

While Freddie and Jim were in Japan, media reports speculating about Freddie's health began to circulate. When they got home, there were journalists waiting for them in the airport asking if Freddie had AIDS. He denied it flatly.

Whether or not Freddie already knew that he was infected, he was already starting to be worried. Two of his ex-lovers had died of the disease, frightening him terribly. At that time little was known about AIDS and, as always with the unknown, it was shrouded with fast-traveling misinformation and much fear. There were those who believed that the virus was directly related to promiscuity, while some media outlets were spreading the notion that AIDS was God's punishment for being gay.

Being HIV-positive meant bearing a stigma that completely changed one's life. Since there was no effective treatment, many people who thought they might be infected didn't even get tested, as confirmation would only add social pressure to the physical symptoms. In those years, a positive diagnosis was, sooner or later, terminal.

Ready to move forward, Freddie got back in touch with Mike Moran in the first days of 1987 to work on an idea he had long wanted to try: a cover of the Platters classic "The Great Pretender." Putting out another artist's song would seem to be unthinkable for the four composing members of Queen, but Freddie followed his hunch.

"The Great Pretender" was originally a love song, but in Freddie's hands it became a declaration of intentions with a much broader meaning. The personas he had created were nothing but a way of pretending, of avoiding presenting himself as he really was. He had invented himself from the beginning of his career, but with this song he distanced himself from the shadow of his character. "The Great Pretender" suggested that he was laying his cards on the table and making his grand confession.

Released in England in February 1987, "The Great Pretender" became his biggest solo record to date, reaching number four on the charts. The single also included a classical composition with Mike Moran on piano, improvised to fill the B-side and called "Exercises in Free Love." Freddie had no way of knowing at the time, but that song was the nucleus of what would be his new solo work, and it would bring him something splendid.

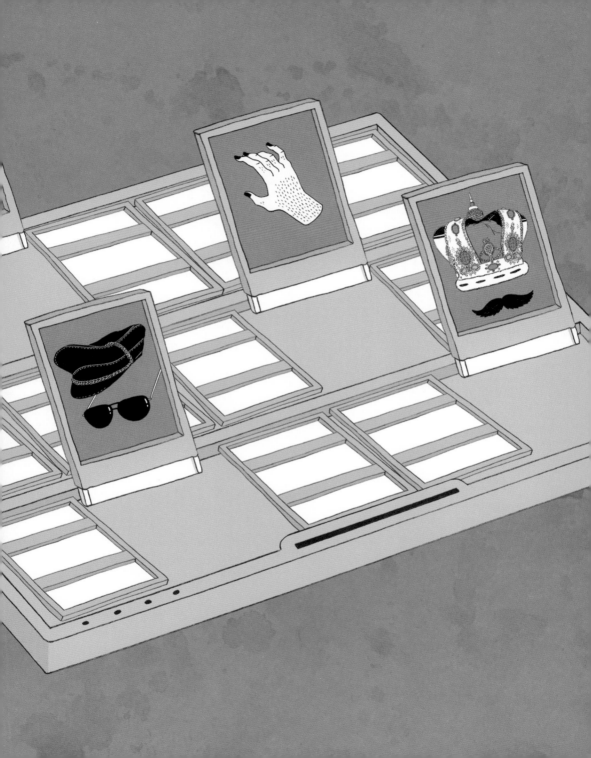

About Freddie's Voice

In 2016, a study by Austrian, Czech, and Swiss scientists demonstrated why Freddie Mercury's voice was practically inimitable. Besides the technical aspects, the study emphasized his incredible vocal range, which reached from a guttural rock-'n'-roll roar to the crystalline tone of his falsetto.

Freddie had never had vocal training apart from being in the school chorus at St. Peter's, so he had no technique to speak of. Moreover, he suffered from a condition called "supernumerary teeth," which, in his case, meant that he had four extra teeth that pushed the rest of his teeth forward. This anomaly mortified him from childhood (and even when he became one the biggest rock stars in the world, he always covered his mouth when he laughed), but he never had oral surgery because he was afraid the change would ruin the way his voice projected.

Not even laryngeal nodes stopped him from singing. Although his vocal cords resented it terribly, he almost never took his doctors' advice to rest his voice.

The year before, when Queen's Magic Tour passed through Spain, a reporter asked Freddie to name his favorite singer. Freddie, normally uncomfortable in interviews, answered easily: Montserrat Caballé.

Freddie admired opera singers for their technical control and their trained voices. He and assistant Peter Freestone had recently attended a performance of Verdi's *Un Ballo in Maschera* at the Royal Opera House of London. As Freddie described it, from the moment Caballé stepped out on stage, he only had eyes for her—because, in his words, "she is music." This declaration didn't take long to reach Caballé's ears. The flattered diva invited Mercury to come meet her in Barcelona.

Their chemistry was immediate. They talked, laughed, and sang until morning. They even improvised on "Exercises in Free Love," the B-side of "The Great Pretender." Both decided that the magic in the air that night in 1986 should be translated into some kind of collaboration. Freddie, enchanted with the idea, proposed that they record a duo. She asked him how many songs a rock album had. "Nine or ten," said Freddie. "Okay, let's do nine or ten," an animated Montserrat answered. Maybe Freddie never got to bring ballet to the masses (as he affirmed in that legendary 1977 interview), but he did bring the rock audience to opera.

From that night on, Montserrat Caballé was "Montsy." Together they began work on Freddie's second solo album. When Jim Beach, the lawyer who at times functioned as Queen's manager, met with the suits at CBS to talk about the record, the company wan't so convinced that it should bet on Mercury again after the way *Mr. Bad Guy* had flopped. They got more interested when they heard that it would be a duet album, and the deal was clinched when Beach told them who the duet partner would be.

Freddie was so excited about this project that no one could talk him out of it; he wanted it to move forward, but by then his health had begun to deteriorate. During a presentation of his second record, *Barcelona*, with Caballé, Freddie was experiencing the early symptoms of AIDS. Some of them, the visible ones, were disguised with makeup that night, but the process was already irreversible.

During the spring of 1987 Freddie had taken a new test that confirmed his HIV infection. At first he just shared the knowledge with Jim Hutton; Joe Fanelli; his assistant, Peter; and his intimate friend Mary. He also told Jim Beach, with the express condition that he not tell the other members of Queen.

Freddie wanted to keep making music with the group: while there was music, there was life.

ROCK

In May 1987, Paul Prenter, Freddie's unscrupulous former assistant, sold an exclusive to the sensationalist daily the *Sun* saying that Mercury had AIDS, and also leaked the news of the death of two of Freddie's ex-lovers from the same disease.

From that moment on, the press was camped outside the front door of Garden Lodge and, although the reporters did not budge from there for years, the singer gave no response other than to deny the media reports.

Freddie, who had never used his private life to get on magazine covers or sell records, found himself in the eye of a media hurricane. Until then he had lived his sexuality in freedom, without any exposure in the media. Having been so closed to the press throughout his career, it was clear that he would give no explanations now.

Although Mercury was deliberately insincere with the media, the rest of the members of Queen lied without knowing it when they were asked about the state of Freddie's health. Maybe they could intuit that something was happening, but at that time they didn't know their bandmates's condition, so they closed ranks to protect his privacy.

The last thing Freddie wanted was to shut himself up at home and waste away. For him, music and life were two concepts that did not exist without each other. The only way not to surrender life was to keep making music. After the release of *Barcelona* in 1988, he got together with the group to record what would be *The Miracle*, Queen's thirteenth album.

That the album cover shows the faces of the band members fusing into one was no accident. During the sessions, the band decided on a show of unity: from then on, the authorship of the songs would be attributed equally to all four members of Queen, slaying the four-headed hydra that had been one of the group's principal sources of conflict. Brian May's lyrics for "I Want It All," one of the album's big hits, took on more meaning in Freddie's voice: "I want it all, I want it now."

When Queen received the Brit Award in 1990 for their contribution to music, Freddie's physical deterioration was evident. Unable to hide it anymore, the singer told the group the truth: "I'm going to talk about this only once," Brian May recalled him saying. "I'm going to tell you what's happening, and after this, I don't want to talk about it any more." He just wanted to keep working, making music until the end.

The group's final studio album, *Innuendo*, released in February 1991, is Freddie Mercury's musical testament. The video for "These Are the Days of Our Lives" is an emotional farewell to his audience, and "The Show Must Go On" is an authentic declaration of intentions. The single's B-side was one of his first hits: "Keep Yourself Alive." There was no song, and no title, more appropriate.

Beyond his music, Freddie left a legacy of strength in his struggle. His message spoke not only to those who suffered the consequences of AIDS, but also to those whose good health allowed them to enjoy every moment of their lives. He showed the world that the virus could affect anyone, whatever their social or sexual status, and his example inspired many to move forward.

In an interview for the documentary *Freddie Mercury: The Untold Story*, Monsterrat Caballé described how Freddie had been honest with her about his health, saying, "I want you to know this because it's my obligation to tell you." To which Montserrat answered, "It's not your obligation to tell me this, but I thank you for having done it, because that signifies that I have your friendship, and that's what matters most to me."

Indeed, Freddie was under no obligation to share his state of health. It wasn't his duty—not as a friend, nor as a public figure—just as he wasn't obliged to reveal any other aspect of his personal life. If he was free to share it, he was also free to reserve it for his intimate friends.

Deciding not to worry about rumors, Freddie ignored the press. Nevertheless, he decided to take advantage of his last days to send a message of normalization and support to a community that was being unjustly stigmatized. On November 22, 1991, he issued a communication that discussed his situation:

> Following the enormous conjecture in the press over the last two weeks, I wish to confirm that I have been tested HIV-positive and have AIDS. I felt it correct to keep this information private to date to protect the privacy of those around me. However, the time has come now for my friends and fans around the world to know the truth, and I hope that everyone will join with me, my doctors, and all those worldwide in the fight against this terrible disease.

While he continued to request that his privacy be respected, Freddie exposed a reality that had to be confronted: the time had come to shine a light into the darkness around AIDS, a darkness that affected not only those infected with the virus but also society as a whole.

Although he had intended to keep composing after the release of *Innuendo*, the moment came when he could scarcely get out of bed. "Mother Love" and "A Winter's Tale," his final compositions, show a fragile Freddie whose strength was ebbing. He had always known that he would keep living as long as he could keep creating music. The moment he realized that that energy was abandoning him, he decided to stop taking his medication.

Two days after sending out his press release, Freddie died at home in Garden Lodge from AIDS-related bronchopneumonia.

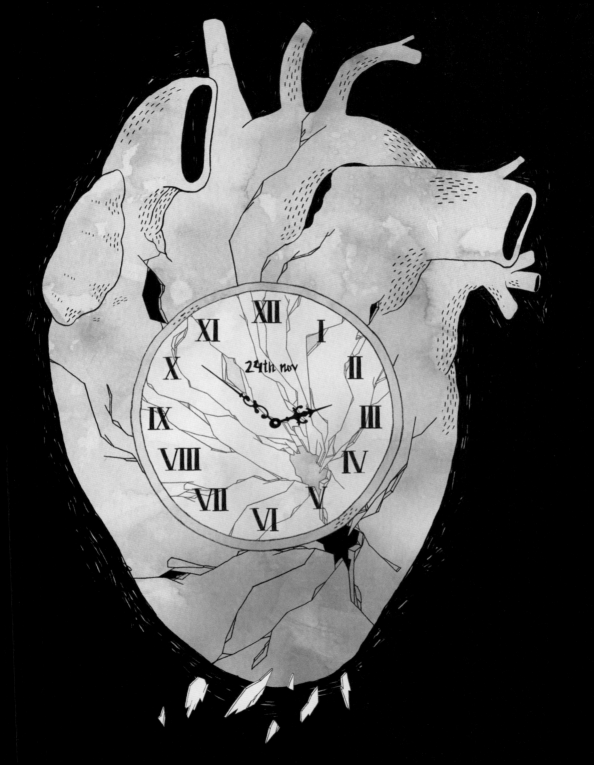

November 24, 1991, was the last time Freddie Mercury was born.

The death of the man was the birth of the legend.

Freddie's funeral, officiated by a Zoroastrian priest, served as a farewell to everyone who knew him and loved him. Hundreds of fans wept for days outside the door of Garden Lodge, which from that moment on became a site of pilgrimage.

In the last stage of his life, Freddie had spent long periods of time in Montreux, Switzerland. Although he had long considered it the most boring city in the world, in his final years he had come to appreciate its tranquility. There a statue was erected in his honor, with an inscription written by Brian May, who demonstrated how well he had known the singer by perfectly condensing into a single phrase Freddie Mercury's life:

Lover of life, singer of songs

Mary Austin took charge of his ashes. Only she knew the exact site where Freddie wanted his remains to rest. Rumors abounded about where the site was, but Freddie wanted it kept a secret, and Mary has respected that wish ever since.

Sometime later, Freddie's will was discovered. Besides giving important sums of money to his assistant, Peter Freestone; to Joe Fanelli; and to his husband, Jim Hutton, Freddie left the lion's share to Mary, who received the artist's house at Garden Lodge and half of the author's rights to the songs. The other half of the author's rights was shared between Freddie's sister and his parents.

To the rest of the world, he left twenty years of songs and one of the most charismatic voices ever.

Darlings, there will not be another like him.

CODA

When Freddie died, the other members of Queen became active in the fight against AIDS, as Freddie had urged in his final communiqué. The reissue of "Bohemian Rhapsody" raised millions for the Terence Higgins Trust, whose funds were earmarked to help HIV-positive people and to search for effective treatment.

Five months after his death, there was a Freddie Mercury tribute concert to raise consciousness about the fight against AIDS.

At Wembley Stadium, great artists like David Bowie, Elton John, Axl Rose, and George Michael bade farewell to Freddie by interpreting the songs of Queen together with the band members. The proceeds of the concert went to the Mercury Phoenix Trust, a charity that today continues the struggle for the eradication of AIDS worldwide.

In one of his last meetings with Jim Beach, Freddie confessed that he had left him nothing in his will, but he left him his music: he could do anything he wanted with it, as long as he didn't do anything boring. Under this authorization, a 1993 remix of "Living on My Own" went to number one on the British charts—Freddie's first number one as a soloist. Along with various compilations of his solo material, his second album, *Barcelona*, was rerecorded with a large orchestra added to Freddie and Montsy's original tracks.

For their part, the members of Queen compiled stray material from the last recording sessions with Freddie, resulting in the 1995 release *Made in Heaven*, which also included tracks from Freddie's solo album. John Deacon definitively left the group after the release of the compilation *Queen Rocks* in 1997, which contained the previously unreleased "No One but You (Only the Good Die Young)," in homage to Freddie. Brian and Roger continue Queen today, which in recent years has been fronted by singers Paul Rodgers and Adam Lambert.

One ongoing annual initiative is Freddie for a Day, in which celebrants disguise themselves in one of Freddie's iconic looks. Every September 5, thousands of Freddies appear in the street all over the world to remind everyone of the importance of the struggle against AIDS.

WELL, THIS
IS OVER . . .

In 1991, the year of Freddie's death, a new asteroid was discovered, which in 2016 was named Freddiemercury 17473. Although Freddie never wanted to go to heaven (he said there would be more interesting people in hell), he would surely have loved this cosmic homage.

Good Bye, Darling.

WHAT HIS SONGS SAY ABOUT HIM

Freddie was one of the main composers of Queen. The numbers tell the story: ten of the seventeen songs in the group's greatest hits collection were his, as were almost half of the singles in the second volume.

Although his musical genres ranged from rockabilly to epic ballad, the theme was always the same. Freddie confessed in various interviews that his compositions didn't probe deep subjects, nor did he write songs with messages like John Lennon did. He only wrote about love and feelings, themes he knew to perfection. He always said that politics should be left to the politicians and that his tunes were instantly enjoyable and immediately disposable, like a T-shirt or a suit you toss because you stopped wearing it. Ironically, Queen wound up with a deep wardrobe closet. Maybe his intention was to create ephemeral songs, but many of his compositions have a place in music history.

Freddie always insisted that there were few or no autobiographical elements in his lyrics. Nevertheless, when we locate each one of his hits in the period in which it was written, we see that they're much more closely related to his life than he wanted to admit—making up a kind of musical biography that demonstrates, once again, that Freddie Mercury lived for and through his music.

SOMEBODY
TO LOVE

In 1976 Freddie Mercury gave up on his romance with Mary Austin and, after being sincere with her, began a new period of his life in which there were many things to discover. And although he had no intention of giving up the freedom he enjoyed at this new stage of his life, after the interminable tours and the long nights, the only thing he wanted was to have someone to share his life with and a home to return to. Freddie always looked for love, but it was hard for him to know if someone coming on to him was sincere. After years of affairs, finally in 1984 he met Jim Hutton, with whom he moved into Garden Lodge. At last he had found what he had so long desired: someone he could love and a beautiful house in which to live together. And cats, lots of cats.

(PLEASE)

"can ANYBODY find me SOMEBODY to love?"

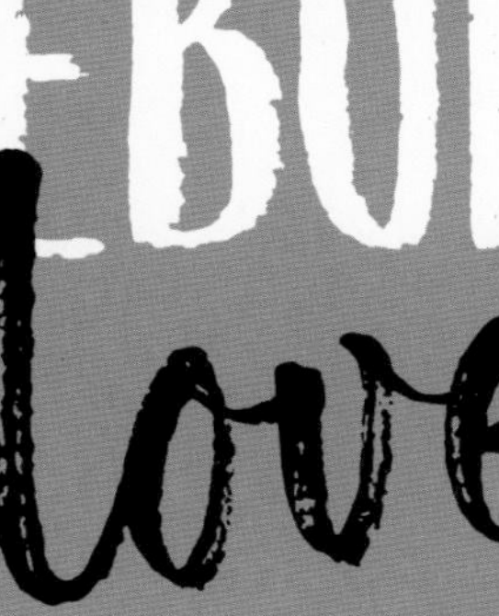

DON'T STOP ME NOW

Brian May, when asked about this song, sometimes says that it transmits a bittersweet feeling. Although the song was a big hit for Queen, it recalls a complicated time for the group and, above all, for Freddie.

In 1978, Mercury was living one of the freest moments of his life: free to love whomever he wanted, free to create, and free to experiment. The late '70s/early '80s were for Freddie a time of excess that the other members of the group viewed with alarm and worry. "Don't Stop Me Now" is Freddie's homage to those years, in which the force of having his own life for the first time propelled him to walk on the wildest side.

"don't stop me NOW I don't want to STOP at all"

MR. BAD GUY

Freddie always tried to stay out of the media spotlight. The music press was not kind to Queen, and he never wanted to feed his private life to the media in any case. Lacking any real information about Freddie Mercury, they created a Freddie out of the details of his stage persona: an arrogant, megalomaniacal character, overly sure of himself, with an inflated self-image as a demigod and a king of rock. Although Freddie was all that and more on stage, it had little to do with the real Freddie.

As the years passed, Freddie kept giving the press what it wanted, feeding the myth of the stuck-up star. Under these conditions, his intimate life was reserved for himself and those he knew best. But there came a moment when he felt himself a prisoner of this persona that he had created. For that reason, when he set to work on his solo album, he decided that *Mr. Bad Guy* would be the title of the album and of one of its songs; in it, he resigns himself to his destiny of wearing the "bad guy" mask that the world has created for him.

"yes I'm
EVERYBODY'S
Mr. Bad Guy
CAN'T you see
I'm
Mr. Mercury?"

THE GREAT PRETENDER

Originally made famous by the Platters in 1955, this song was obviously not written by Freddie Mercury, though it fit him so well that it could have been.

Although it was originally a love song, as sung by Mercury it takes on new nuances. Whereas in "Mr. Bad Guy" he admits to wearing a disguise that doesn't represent him, in "The Great Pretender" he removes the disguise, presenting himself to the world as a big phony who pretends to be what he's not. In this song, the Freddie character removes layer after layer, only to discover that beneath all the disguises, there's only a normal man who one day decided that pretending to be a strong person was almost the same as being one. The game of mirrors came to an end with the release of this song.

(OOH YES)

"I'm the great
PRETENDER
I seem to be
what
I'm NOT"

ACKNOWLEDGMENTS

Some years ago, when we were first dating, we were immersed in one of those conversations in which you try, in equal measure, to show who you are and at the same time impress the other a little. That day, talking about music between laughs and beers, you asked me: "What singer, now dead, would you have liked to have seen in concert?"

I don't remember exactly what I answered, but I know I asked you the same thing. You paused to take a sip of your beer (maybe that didn't happen, but that's how I remember it), and you said: "Freddie Mercury." There's no better answer, I thought, taking that as a signal.

Years after those first dates, the conversations are different. Now they're about the shopping list or our vacation plans, but now I know that the answer to that innocent question was one of the first things we discovered we had in common.

To you, and to all your family, I dedicate this book.

BIBLIOGRAPHY

Books and Blogs

Blake, Marc. *Freddie Mercury. A Kind of Magic*. Barcelona: Editorial Blume, 2016.

May, Brian. "Happy birthday, Freddie Mercury." Googleblog.blogspot.com. https:// googleblog.blogspot.com/2011/09/happy-birthday-freddie-mercury.html.

Mercury, Freddie. *Freddie Mercury, su vida contada por él mismo*. Barcelona: Robinbook, 2007.

O'Hagan, Sean. *Freddie Mercury, una vida en imágenes*. Barcelona: Libros Cúpula, 2013.

Documentaries

Bird, Christopher, dir. *Queen: Rock the World*, 2017.

Dolezal, Rudi, and Hannes Rossacher, dir. *Freddie Mercury: The Untold Story*, 2000.

Fothergill, John, dir. *The Freddie Mercury Story: Who Wants to Live Forever*, 2016.

Johnston, Carl, dir. *The Story of Bohemian Rhapsody*, 2004.

Longfellow, Matthew, dir. *Queen: A Night at the Opera*, 1997.

O'Casey, Matt, dir. *Queen: Days of Our Lives*, 2011.

Smeaton, Bob, dir. *Is This Real Life?*, 1999.

Thomas, Rhys, dir. *Freddie Mercury: The Great Pretender*, 2012.

This
book was first
published, in Spanish,
at the end of the first days of
September 2018.

Freddie would have turned
seventy-two.

This is our little birthday
present for him.